The Point of No Return

BOOK I

———————— • ————————

PHILOMA NOEL

outskirts
press

Outskirts Press, Inc.
http://www.outskirtspress.com

ISBN: 978-1-9772-2174-2

ACKNOWLEDGEMENTS

My perseverance derives from the love of God in my life. For me that means Goodness, mercy and the people of God, who have loved me for more than I deserve. Without the Lord Jesus Christ, I would still be seeking directions and purpose instead of inspiring others to keep pressing onward. Grace also means being a pastor to the greatest family on earth, the family of God now for almost three years. Moving forward means an awesome wife and children in your corners through every situation you can think about. If all wives and children were like mine, fewer husbands and dads would be down and out. My two oldest are out and about doing and pursuing their careers and goals. They are venturing new areas, but I feel sure in the faith that the investments made in them by the grace of God, will be the stability of their times. I am blessed and thankful for that beautiful daughter my God saw fit to give my wife and me.

I am indebted to a host of faithful man and women who have influenced my concepts of determination. Among them are Pastor Woolly Doriscar, Pastor Glenn Walker, Pastor Albert Adams and Pastor Gennaro Russo. Without these women, my mom, stepmom, Flavy Zizi, and Dieudonne Joseph, My life would not be as productive as it is today. I think God for my favorite principal, Angie Taillon who when they asked, "why him?" she said, "He's it!"

They have played a key role in the shaping and molding of my life as it is today. I am forever grateful for Monica Harman editorial expertise and team for helping me meet publication deadline and guidelines. Last, and most important, I want to express my gratitude to the hundreds of people who are going to be changed by the purchasing and reading of this inspirational. This book is the first to many to come and a tribute to their desire to move onward.

Introduction

This is a story of my life's experience with God the father, creator of heaven and Earth. I clearly stated the true identity of God because, we all live in a world where there are many counterfeiters humanity has created to represent God, but they are not the mighty God; they are not the everlasting Father or the Prince of peace. I pray and hope that this quantification of my thoughts, through the inspiration of the Holy Spirit will trigger your heart, mind and soul to understand the breadth and width of both the knowledge and love of God. I pray that this inspiration will propel you, the reader, to search and stay on course with God in a greater and deeper magnitude which will change individual lives toward an intimacy with the true creator of the universe.

So let's see, as far as I could remember, I find myself in the island of Haiti; as if it was just yesterday.

Children playing near the monumental Citadel and oh the good days of child hood. I remember the joy of eating fresh grabbed of a juicy mango from the mango tree. Haiti was good to me. I was not born in Haiti, for according to my birth certificate and testimony of both my mom and dad, I was born in the tropical island of the Grand Bahamas where the palm trees were green with so much life.

I don't quite know why I used tropical, but it sounded good in my finite mind. To continue and to be more precise, I was born in Freeport, Grand Bahamas. While my parents were struggling in their relationships, my mom thought, for the safety and well being of my brother and me, she took us to Haiti. While there, my grandparents and Auntie took over the caring and nurturing of my older brother, sister and cousins. As much as I hated being separated from my mom, now in my late forties, I realized the favor, the character building during that time and plan and purpose of God for me through that period of endless frustrations in my life. This was a **point of no return**. God orchestrated my life even before I was born in my mother's womb.

He knew and "knows my name" one writer specified. So true, the great "I Am" does take care and is mindful in the affairs of men. The Potter has and still do shape the potteries even today. I am one of those vessels changed and still being formed into his perfect plan. The Majesty is still melting and molding me into his

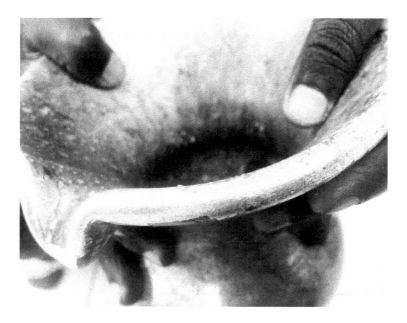

POINT OF NO RETURN

Likeness, today. I am not who I'm supposed to be, but little by little and day by day he is changing me into an incredible masterpiece. So don't you be discouraged if you're not there yet because we are all beauty in the making.

Sometimes, we doubt the outcome of the master's hand, but we need to be patient he's not through with us yet. I am not sure, whatever his plans are, we have come too far. It is the **point of no return**.

To continue, while in Haiti, for about 6 or 7 years, I experience many hardships. I went through neglects and abandonments, but through it all, my God never left me. My brother and I, prior to being with my grandparents, experienced disappointments and harsh treatments at the hands of, what we would call today, a foster parent. She received funds from my mom, I was told, but did not spend it on us. After a year or two with her, somehow, my dear grandparents gave us a surprise visit which also caught our foster parent off guard. My grandparents investigated our living quarters and physical wellbeing and realized that it was unsuitable. Because of this fact, they decided it was time we moved North of Haiti to be with them. It was the best thing that could have happened to my brother and me. Life was never the same. I began to experience love and family. I had a paradigm shift in my life. A change I did not know would take place, ever. I had brothers and a sister I did not know were there. I had cousins galore; life was changing for the better in a way my little mind could not conceived, but this was God's plan from the beginning. He was shaping me so that I may glorify him and him alone. How could I have known that this big, big God had such an awesome plan for me, but he does for each and every one of us. This was the beginning of my **point of no return**. A life sealed and delivered from my God and God alone.

As I turned nine or ten years old, I remember sitting outside with a group of friends. We were flying our kites on a beautiful sun shining day. The skies were bright and the wind was blowing. As I looked to the skies, sitting on that clay and dirt mound, I noticed as if the clouds in the skies were unusually, vocal. As I gazed into the skies above, I was amazed at God's creation. In my heart was this thought, there must be a God up there. As I thought about that, it seems that, though I did not know it, I was approaching a **point of no return**. From the time we were little until now, like a little child, God has been there to keep and nurture us. My father in heaven was communicating with me through his creation, his splendor and such a unique way unknown to me at first. Wow he care so much for us, we really cannot tell it all. God was beginning to reveal himself little by little as I can take.

POINT OF NO RETURN

Being in an island filled with superstitions, witchcrafts and chaos, my God covered me from it all. In 1980 or 81, my aunt, Augustine by the grace of God, saw the need to bring me back to the United States. My mom later stated it was because of her I was back in the US. Apart from the subject and purpose of the matter, God was still in control. Bless my beautiful mom's heart and rest her soul. To continue, as I arrived to the United States, I finally got the chance to be united with my mom again. It was joy everlasting. Wow, I said while plunging my teeth for the first time into a whopper from Burger king which I care none for now. Look what I was missing! Am I in heaven? And if so, leave me there! Nevertheless, it was bitter and sweet at the same time. It was sweet because I was enjoying this fine food, I thought, while families in Haiti were not. It was sweet because I am united with my mom and oldest brother, Eric again. Yes, my oldest brother, Eric, was my trainer on how to fight and yes he was also my protector in the town in Haiti. He showed me how to defend myself. And if I didn't defeat my opponent, it was embarrassment somehow more for him than me! Yes, here I was once again with my brother; it was amazing and just really cool seeing him again. Another reason being in the states was sweet is that I had a younger sister I didn't know about. I felt happy but not complete because I missed my family back home in the island of Haiti. But being in the United States was also bitter because I was eating well and love ones were not. I thought of Grandma and Pa which was my Grandpa. I'd ponder on their wellbeing almost all the time. Health wise, are they ok? And will I ever see them again. To my surprised, a year later, I received an unpleasant surprise. You see I had never known my biological father. The concept of a father to me was my granddaddy, so when my mom introduced a new man in my life, I did not know how to react. I was like, ok… Nevertheless, I was again at a **point of no return**. I verbally accepted what was, but deep down, I was in denial. But as I look back, once again, God is the master craftsman. He is the great engineer at work. He drew our plans well even when it is beyond our comprehension. The apostle Paul said, everything will work together for our good. From one event to another; if you love God, and you are the call to his purpose, your steps will be ordered by him. Take refuge in your God. David stated, in psalms 27, and so even when your father or mother by any means, forsake you, he said God will take you up. Isn't that the truth? Our good Lord self said, in Deuteronomy 31: 6, "he will never leave us nor forsake us". I tried him and found him to be all that and more. **I'm at a point of no return**. Now I've allowed you take a trip in my time capsule, my journey from here to yonder, but it is only the beginning. God has proven his unfailing love over and over in my life. As the writer stated so eloquently, "what is man that thou art so mindful of him". That's right! If we take the time, we can see the ordering of God's love all over and over again in our lives. He is the faithful one even when we are not. Isn't that correct? He is patient and everlasting. A God who never fails and he is so good at what he does.

God is great and greatly to be praise. I won't turn back by the grace of God. In a world where good is evil and evil is good, I will hold on to the unfailing hand. It is my **point of no return.** After you have tried them all, and they were all lies, strengthens your tied with your God.

He will take you deeper and wider than any have gone before. His thoughts concerning us are good and not evil. He wants to give us an expected end. Don't be discouraged when you are in the master's hand. He intends to take you through and bring you out. He is beyond measure! Truthfully, who can compare with him? Get ready! Trust in him because when you think all is about to be the worst, it is when it's about to get good. No matter what you're going through. He'll make it alright. He did for me and it is getting even better. Stay in the game and don't throw in the towel. you are at the **point of no return**. It is a point in time in your life where God has proven time and time again that he knows your ups and your downs. He does know and cares about you. He is not going to ignore his beloved. You are chosen by him before you knew it. Way, and way back and back! You were on his mind before He was on your mind. Yep! The great God and creator of the Universe had you and me on his mind. Oh yes! Oh yes! Can you believe this? We are children of the King of kings. Where was I?

Ok, so here I am once again united with my mom and a brand new dad. Can you believe it? I should be happy, right? I was all in the mix and confused but not God though. You and I have a maker. Oh yes and he formed our every coarse in life. You can believe it. Regardless of what you are going through and will go through, it will work out for your good. When it is hard, do not look back! Don't murmur or complain why it's not someone else. You're chosen for such a time as this. You are at the breaking point of your life. You can break for the good of all men or break yourself from achieving your purpose. Yes, you can hander yourself from fulfilling your role in life. That's right; it is your **point of no return**. There is an awesome psalmist in the Bible. He was in the flesh but currently in the spirit and well. From the beginning of his life, God had proven time and time again, He was with him. God through historic strengths and miracles in his life had proven that he is his anointed. Before he knew his calling and purpose by God, situations in his life had proven that there was a greater destination ahead. This man time and time again, if he had eyes to see, would have realized that Jehovah God was with him. This awesome writer, according to the holy word, "a man after God's own heart" was David. What about you and me? I realized that we often failed to roll back the curtains of memories now and then. We failed to see where he brought us from and where we are today. Because of this fact, we complain and go back to the mud. We lay there and forget the greater plan. We become blinded by the muddy situations of life. We become comfortable and think, oh what a life or life is just stink!. I might as well enjoy my destiny and join the crowd of lost purpose and vision of the creator. We take a detour and enter what I call, the bear mode. I eat and eat as many berries of life that I can. Whether good or bad, I am just tired of life. The fallen nature is taking its course on me and I think I just got to go with the flow. There is no need to fight or struggle. Just loosen up man! I go into hibernation. I sleep to God and alive to the nature of things. I give in and believe this is it for me. You see, I was like that. I use to drift like a wood on a stream; I was like chaff floating in the wind. I was as the wind blows so I took it. I really had no sense of direction; I had no purpose and no goal. I was drifting down stream, endlessly. Whatever came or whatever went I was down with it. I was cool but one day, the master again revealed himself to me. I was once again, maybe 12. Eric, my oldest brother, had a good friend named let say, Gary. Gary invited him to a picnic and I had the privilege of tagging along. To my surprised, Gary treated me as if I was his son. He never knew me and I never knew him. Gary was a white man of God in spirit and in truth. He picked me up and carried me on his shoulder. This was a **point of no returned** for me. My great God was showing me something here. He knew I would need this background for my future relationships. Until this day, I never forget this big white brother caring and placing me on his shoulder. This move by God revealed that he has no respect of person. That in every color or race, if we call and accept him he will carry us through life's unforgettable situations. Have there been some unforgettable occasions where we have failed to see the almighty's guiding hand? He was there all along and carried you through your storm of life. Have there been some unbearable situations that you know it wasn't and it just could not have been you who brought you through? You see I have done that but now I am at a **point of no return**. Yes from the big white brother Gary, to my brother introducing me to God by going to church with him, my life was changing.

Still I did not know to what extent, but the master had me in his hand. What am I suggesting to you? I am asking you not to cut your walk with God short. Don't do shipwreck! Stay afloat and on the boat to greater and bigger tomorrow. Fear not for the Lord thy God is with thee. He said, "I will not leave thee nor forsake thee". Why worry or afraid; the Lord hadn't failed you as others have and will do. Makeup your mind and trust and believe. There is a brighter day up ahead. Do not let doubts of divers forms reside in your thoughts and intents of your heart. "Be not deceived; evil communication corrupts good manners". You know that your God has called you and no weapon formed against you shall prosper. No matter how hot and humid it gets. Gold has to go through deep and deep pressure to shine. That's who we are in the middle of whatever; the Lord's endeavors are to make us more than conquerors through him. You are at your **point of no return**. Your destination is good not evil; be expecting to be the head and not the tail; I declare the children of God, lenders and not borrowers. Don't look back for self pity. Disregard any invitations from self doubt and deceit. Put away descent to inferiority and sadness of neglect, but roll back to see where he has brought you from only to press onward to brighter you in your God. He is about to turn it around for you. The good Lord has brought you from a mighty, mighty long way. Don't throw in your towel. Use it only to wipe the sweat off the brow. Let the blood stain banner raised high and let the enemies of your soul know that greater is he that is in you than he that is out there. You are the righteousness of God. You are kings and priest and you will fulfill the glory of him who called you out of darkness into his marvelous light. This is your **point of no return**. Lift your eyes unto the hills child of God from whence your help cometh from; you will find that it comes from nobody else, but God. I have found him to be constant and amazing. Oh yes! That is his name. He is truly an everlasting father to the fatherless. Remember the man after God's own heart? He said in Psalms 27:10,"when my father and mother forsake me, then the LORD will take me up". What an assurance David had. After his many trials and tribulations in his life, he failed not to recognize the sovereign hand constantly guiding and protecting him from the storms and manifold situations life can bring. Are you in the cleft of the Rock? Are you under the shadows of his wings? If not make him your hiding place from the whirlwinds of life. No matter what spin life may bring, please stay in the ring. In spite of it all, even when your back's against the wall. Stand tall. Our God will not let us fall. The book of Matthews states, "if any man would here these sayings of mine, and doeth them, I will liken him as a Wise man, which build his house on the Rock:

And the rain descended, and the floods came, and the winds blew, and beat upon that house; and it fell not: for it was founded upon the Rock".

POINT OF NO RETURN

What is your foundation made of? If it's Christ you're built on, than you're on solid ground. Everything else in life is just sinking sand. They shift unexpectedly. Nothing else in life can hold us through the sticky and profound situations of life like God can. Stay in the arms of the everlasting for you are on the brink of a new day. You're at your **point of no return.** "You can bank on it;" somebody once told me. Situations may come to try you, but don't think that this is something strange happening to you or this should not be happening. Don't say you are worthless or forgotten by God. No! It is a sign that you are a child of God. This exact situation(s) are designed to reveal to you that you are received by God. That is crazy right? I learned that though we go through the fire, it will not burn us. Are you kidding me, you might be thinking about now. Remember this child of God, as it was for the Hebrew boys, only the things that bound us, will burn in our trials. My troubles only came to make me stronger. Though it may be hard, do like the three Hebrew boys, rejoice for you are not alone. Every bit of bruises and knock downs, though you may be thrown down, remember this, you are not alone. You are at your **point of no return.** Don't look back Jack and just strap on because you were born for success and not stress. You are a child of the risen King. Sling-shot positive hopes forward into your appointed destination station. Wipe those tears of your eyes. You are heirs with Christ and Joint heirs with God. Rise and take your place in the kingdom of God for you are about to embarked on a great journey. Remember those lions and bears of life God gave you? Also remember, He's also given you strengths to defeat them. Oh yes you can do it. Remember, not by your might or power but it will always be by his spirit! This is your **point of no return**.

Point of no return

What a mighty God we serve and most of the time we don't deserve his love and mercy. Though we doubt him time and time again, he stays forever faithful. Though we fail him, he specializes and creating in us a master piece. That's right! He is the great architect and potter of our lives. Transforming this inexcusable hunk of clay into the image of his dear son. Most of the time we work against the will of the great father and master lover of our soul. We hardened up and refused to be used. But with his gentle spirit he softens our abusive nature little by little into his likeness. John says, "it may not yet appears what we shall be;" thank you Lord! I am so glad that the potter is patient with the clay. This is the **point of no return.** It is a very important curve so don't change lane. There are dangers that can be ignored if we allow the potters hand to melt and mold us into a vessel that is fit for his plan. The choice is up to me and you. I have reached that point and time. A master piece or a cracked pot, it's all up to me if I allow the process of the potter and the clay to take place. Then there will be hope for me and you as clay in the potters' hand. Clay pot is a process that requires endurance. God is taking us, a lump of supposed to be soft clay, but we are in contrary, hard by nature. He throws us onto a revolving wheel. That's his church where his ministry on earth through his spirit begins the molding process in some other way, until it takes on the shape that he wants it to have. The intent is that the next form we take, if the potter which is God is happy with the result, he decides to decorate it, and then a pot, you are me is ready for the fathers bidding. But if he is not happy with the result, God in is mercy simply will mash the clay with water again, and then start the process again. Do you see the process of our incredible God? Do you see the love of God in our life? We could have been thrown away with the other crackpots of life, but God in his love and mercy, rewrote our lives. Child of God, you are at a **point of no return**.

That is just amazing to me. If I were the potter, that's fine, ofcourse. I would be in command. But what if I was the lesser of the two? That's more interesting. The harmony between the potter and the clay or pot is truly intimate. The potter or master craftsman is the hands of God or creator. I have a couple of mugs which, at first, looks like a perfectly fine mug. Probably, you would think, there are hundreds of identical ones around, coming off the different factories at some pottery. But you would be wrong! Some of those mugs are hand-made mugs, produced by the very hand or ministering spirits of God. Some of us have had many hands, directed by the spirit of God, melting in molding us. We have experience changes from here, there and all around the world. People and programs have shaped our lives in more ways than one. What is so special and unique is that no two pots will be identical. No matter if we are twins or whatever. It you look carefully, and you will see that you have a specify purpose for your life. That's right! You are the only one of your model and made with a specific purpose by the master and creator. You have been shaped and there are marks of greatness all over you. You belonged to the Master of the Universe. He is the potter making you. There's no turning back now for you are at the **point of no return**. Lift your eyes to the hills from whence your help cometh from, your help cometh from the maker and potter, our God himself. Be encourage, no matter what your going through. He'll make it alright, but you got to stay strong! He said he will never turn his back on you. You belong to him and him alone. Stay on the ship and no evil will come near you and yours. You are a chosen generation and one destined for great things. Is there anything to hard for your God to do for you? Hasn't he proven time and time again the he can and will do it for you. Whatever you've asked in his name he is able to do above that. I am so persuaded that there is nothing impossible to our mighty and most powerful God. We are moving forward and no turning back friend. You are the chosen one and your life is in his hand. Keep all positive thoughts in the bus now. Closed every window of doubts. All ifs and buts are not allowed. Let all unbelief be given a notice of evacuation. They have caused enough turbulence and uneasy feelings on your plan of departure. You would have flown high but your passengers are dead weights. You must lay aside every weights and sin that so easily hold you down. Press on to the mark and anchor our Lord Jesus Christ. This is our **point of no return**. It is a point that only those who trust in the Lord with all their hearts get to. It's a turn that acknowledgements must be completely on the good Lord. You cannot make it on your own at this rough sea. The winds are too strong and ragging alone. You need the master of the sea to overcome the tempest in the deep. I found that they who trust and remained under his wings and shadow of the Almighty will not be put to shame. My God has taken me from nothing and is turning my stumbling block into a stepping stone. I am not worthy of anything that the Lord has done for me. He has taken a sinful boy destine for nothing into something beautiful. He has changed one who had no hope into a vessel of honor. My life has been inspired to lead and change others into a similar relationship of honor and glory. The master craftsman has done this by his power. I now understand the process of the master's hands. It is so kind and comforting. Taking us the lump and working it until it is acceptable. Rely on the master's hands friends; he specializes in things that seem impossible. It does not matter

PHILOMA NOEL

our background or pedigree. He is the best and without him we can do nothing. As we are learning to lean and breathe in him or allow him to breathe in us life and that more abundantly, we will achieve great and mighty things. Be encourage my sisters and brothers, the master has an amazing closure to our mess and you will be bless. I never thought I would be serving God's people in such a magnitude. I'm leading God's people by his grace in this race and it is just a humbling experience. As his hands through the ministries of my upbringing, now he is using me to melt and mold his next generational pots in the same way. It is such a privilege. One that is sacrificial and so humbling. He did not have to use my life but he did. I am so undeserving of this honor but my God has turned someone I would not have chosen into something beautiful. A life blessed by his wonderful people every day. See, this is now **a point of no return**. A life admonished by his spirit and motivated by his love for his people in my life. God has never seemed to amaze me. He is truly wonderful to me. My mind cannot conceive the depth of God. Truly he is unsearchable and really incredible. I am finding out, if you lean on him and draw closer to God, he is only a thought or breath away. Before you ask, he will answer.

POINT OF NO RETURN.

What an omniscient God. He has all knowledge and capability in his hands. The whole world and Universe is a drop in a bucket for him. And he is mindful of us. He takes time, this great creator of this huge and enormous world, to care for little old you and me. What a mighty God we serve. The one angels bow down before him has taken the time to hear our every prayer. That is so magnificent to me. This is why I've come to this **point of no return.** It is a hiding place in God, where no foul can build nest on my head. It is a place of comfort but not complacency. It is a place of unending possibilities and excitements. It is a place of encouragements and doubtless courage in the God that is able to fulfill what he has said. No, I won't go back to me, myself and I. It is a point of unresolved issues and disappointments. I will not seek for satisfactions of the past rebukes and resentments. I am moving onward! It is a place, a tangible place of safety and security.

It's a place that only God can reach our hearts and souls. It's a place of beauty and unending inspirational wealth. It is a place where the "son" never stops to shine.

It is a place of acceptance and a path leading to life in every step that I take. It is a brighter path of knowledge and understanding of who God is and what he requires of me and his people. It is a place where discouragements and division prone characters are of the past. It is a drive on the positive of the word and inspiration of the spirit of God. It is based on the fruits of the spirit and not lust of the flesh. This new path brings a good conscience towards my God and savior Jesus Christ. I won't go back by his grace because he has brought me a mighty long way. I am on the **point of no return.**

Point of no return

Have you ever wondered what it would be liked without the potters' hands? To me it is the worst feeling ever. I'd be lost and pointless in a deep black hold with no way out, ever. A speck of dust in my eye, unpleasantly there and annoying. A meaningless life without any purpose. Life would just seem hopeless, but God saw it fit to change me and rearrange me. Though I have tried, but my words and intent of my heart will never be able to express my deepest thoughts about the work that God has done and is doing in my life. I am bless and highly favored of God. A piece of clay turned vessel of honor for the masters' great house. What a wonderful thing just to know that he really loves me, as the song said, "just to think of who he is and who I am." I am so glad that he chose me out of all that he could have used, another writer wrote. So now I want to give him my heart and soul for he is too wonder then my soul can phantom. A great and mighty God saw it fit to reconstruct a piece of clay and made it into something beautiful of my life.

This is the time; it is my point of no return and your life is too!
The world is waiting and is in your hands.

PHILOMA NOEL

A life driven and destined to achieve the greatness of the Lord in all that I do. He is my guide and compass so I was made to look forward no matter what. We are made in his image, the likeness of the God of the universe. He will always be the unchanging and unending God. Beside him there is no other. Life will come at you with all sorts of interrupting obstacles and confusions to stir you adrift but looking to the author and finisher of your faith and success should be the aim. We must not look back for there is nothing behind but sorrow and disappointment. To be like him in every way, is to begin with the outcome in mind. The desires of your heart will not come to pass unless you desire to forget anything that does not resembles your future and gains. I must forget those things which are behind me and press forward, daily. It is a constant effort to proclaim the fame or victory. One must keep in mind that this surmountable his will not be given to just the swift, but to him or her that has endurance flowing to her very being. Victory will be given to those constantly leaning forward with every bit of efforts and sacrifice. One must have a made up mind. It is a determination that surpasses all procrastination. This is a **point of no return**. It is a point of pain, yet above ground of high elevations and gains. At this destination, ones heart is constantly throbbing under strong stress but one has gone too far. You just don't know it but the victory lap is closer than before.

It is amazing and understanding, life at times can really make you doubt the conclusions of your desired dreams and aspirations, but we must gather self and hold on to that inner drive and strengths in God. Don't lose faith in the author of dreams and reality. This route that you are on is made for the strong and determined. You are about to make it in just a little while. Be strong and cast a side doubts and debris of life. People, objects and cares of life will hinder your view of your paths. Be determined and focus on what's ahead. Your eventuality is only a mile away. All that you have worked for isn't far at all. It is just over there and around the corner. Can't you see it? Just hold on and encourage yourself. You've worked so very persistent and oh the calories you have burned. It is your season to reap what you have sown. Everything is working exactly for your good. You may not noticed or understand just yet, but it is going to get clearer soon. The clouds are moving out of your sky. Soon what appeared or was grey will be blue because the son, that's right, the son of righteousness is about to show himself strong on your behalf. Don't you look back and contemplate ifs and buts. You are destined for resolutions of the greatest kind, a life of no regrets and disappointments. God has proven time and time again that he is on the throne and is at home. We just failed to remember his strong arm in and around us. He brought us from such a mighty long way. This is a **point of no return**. Too many miles behind us and too many rivers our feet have crossed through to look back now.

Be encouraged no matter what you're going through. He'll make it all right, but you have to stay on the track. Stay in that lane of narrow but life giving opportunity for you and everyone associated with you. Be determined to succeed, not just for you, but for you and yours and generation after you. We have those born and on the verge of coming in our time and place. Our accomplishments are not just for self, but for lives after and after. Here and there and everywhere, people those on their way will need guidance and a light to succeed. That shine from the lighthouse will come from our accomplishments and focus on the future generations. Our visions and thrive, must not only focus on us but for those to come. We are born to dominate a system that is determined to cause those who are called today to falter in the path that will lead to the wellbeing of many to come. We were not born just for self indulgence, but for multiplication and continuation of generations to come. We were born as those before, for the thriving of future posterities. Isn't this a life worth striving for? Partaking in such a quest is a blessing beyond our greatest imagination. To conquer doubts and disappointments and to realize that the vision of my life is much greater than what I longed for in life. Life is not merely about a four, eight or 12 year goals, but its way and way beyond that. It is a life driven by a creator to resolve a purpose above purpose not realized by everyone. Though signs and directions are given but most ignored by selfish ambitions. Guidance and support are given in many ways than one. Don't look back at misfortunes as a negative because for the elect and chosen, every situation is a chance to be refined for the long haul. It is your due season. You just don't know that you are in the making. Your name has been called and you just than hear it. Pay attention to the next sign ahead. They are there purposefully to direct your path to the point of arrival. Be careful in how you're accepting the thoughts of your inner you.

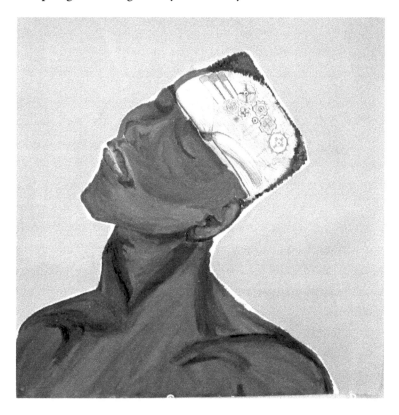

At this point, self is the greatest obstacle in your route to glory. Oh you might get tired up this steep hill but don't worry, others have a mountain to climb. It may seem at times lonely but look towards that hill because your help will come from on high not below. Don't look down but face whatever may come at you. You have that ability to do the impossible. You are that next contestant on the price is right. Just hang in there because this is your **point of no return**. Your destination is closer than when you first begun. There's no stopping you now for the road ahead is about to get clearer and brighter into a perfect sun shining day. Lookout now, you are on the right course to redemption of battles you did not believe you can win, but look at you now. Pickup you head and realize that what is for you is for you. Deep down inside you know it, even when it hurts. You were born for this; in your genes are the DNA for insurmountable heights in God. Heights you never conceived before, but it is for you and others like you. You were called for this and that and so much more. Regardless of what it may look like, life situations don't dictate what you are going to be. Explore your new horizon with confidence and know for a fact that nothing can stop you but self. You are your worst enemy. That's right, your enemy and friend is you and no one else. Put your thoughts and excuses on hold, daily. Our greatest walls of delusions are the ones within. They are walls that have been constructed by situations and circumstances of best to forget relations.

Some foundations were laid by, sadly, love ones. Nevertheless, anything that causes struggles and deadweights must be dropped off along the way. hay will burn when the situations get hot and unbearable, so it is time to go alone and not holding on and picking up unwanted passengers that will drain the life out of you. Situations and habits can and will do that. Your goals and aspirations will not be resolve if one is bearing bad news and ill and resentful luggage. Drop off despairs and sadness. Let go of reproach and self-pity. This is your time of restitution; this is your **point of no return**. You were made for this and nothing can stop you now. Base every circumstance as a mean to bring you closer to your destination. You are gold and these elements on your way are designed to chip and clean you thoroughly. They are there to brighten every areas of your life that you become fit for any eventuality. This is your show and your hour of success. Embrace every opportunity as your own and don't take anything personal. Smile in the middle of your situations and don't shy away from any turbulence in your way. This is your season to reap everything you have sown. It may seem that way but you are not alone on this journey. Your creator and master of the universe is not going to leave you comfortless. You were born for this and nothing can stop you now. Every arena has been set to create in you a protagonist, a warrior and powerful soldier of truth and principle. You are that one that will make the difference for many to come, so be lifted up. Truthfully, there is none specifically like you. You are unique and well designed for success of many to come so claim your fame. I'm persuaded that nothing can separate us but self. That's why great exercises like reading the bible and communicating with the right people will break you or make you. The choice is ours to make at any given time. We should not be deceive by self and others, but I want to emphasized on self most importantly because out of our own hearts lies deceit and ill messages that will detour us from the path of life.

In us lies wickedness that can stir the heart and mind into unforgiving destruction of many. One must be vigilant and wise as the viper. Standing watch daily is imperative to count-less lives here and there. It's time to awake and conquer the

PHILOMA NOEL

tricks and pits of the enemy inner me. This is the **point of no return**.

In a world where disappointments are like floods, and when it seems that our lives are constantly turning in a whirlwind, always remember that tests and trials are but for a moment. Though it seems forever, the "son" will shine again. "Weeping may endure for a night but joy will come in the morning". I am so learning to forbear and hold on in the toughest periods of my life now. This was not always the case. No! I had not always been positive and so confident that everything is going to work out. It took time and experience with our God and savior to bring me to the **point of no return** and what a destination. This is such a peaceful place where doubts still come but I do not open my heart and ear gates to listen. I heard enough about how I can't and will not make it. I am tired of the idea that only he or she can but this is not for you. I don't compromise with my deficiencies of the past anymore. No this took time to develop. It required a metamorphic process in my life. I had to get a growth mind change. I had to have a paradigm shift. My surrounding had to change naturally and spiritually. One cannot encourage change without a move. And sometimes, it is going to require a radical move of the third kind. A drastic move that most will not understand but it does not matter. It is not about him or her but it is about you. It's about your future and those around you. It is your **point of no return**. It is and will be a lonely road at times but that's ok. Many of the great ones past and to come will have to walk that road to accomplish the purpose for their lives. That is right; we, you and me do have a very important role to play in this path that we are on. We are not bench warmers. But when I think about it, even the bench warmers have a very important part. They must be great supporting cast and observant. They must be if not a complete but close enough to the image of the leader or leaders to provide necessary help in time of need. That's very critical so yes even the seemingly passive members are at the end very important to the benefit and well being of the team and or family. No one is an island to self. We all need to work and synergize. It is what make the machines work and team wins. Synergy! Don't look at what you need but look at what you have been given. You're better than you think or believe that you are. Use what's in your hands. Your talent and gift is not like any other. You are created with purpose and care. Similar to every string of hair or particles in the air, the master knows you from beginning to end. You are unique and no one is identical to you. Fulfill your mission by not attending to procrastination. Rise and see your potential and take the initial, step. Only you can stop you. This is your **point of no return.** As long as you are breathing and have your being, nothing can stop you. You are just getting started. The world is waiting for you to lead and inspire.

Is yourself talking negatively to you again. Don't listen. Close the door and do more, with you. Haven't you heard yet? Many books have not been written. Many movies are not yet directed. And many other inventions haven't been created. Do you know why? Some have taken the lesser road. Many have returned to the woe is me status. Many have claimed to be the self designee, victim of past generational inadequacies. But not you though, you are better than that. You are way smarter than that. Your past will not and cannot define who you are going to be, negatively. But you are going to take your past and turn every stumbling block into a stepping stone. You are going to rise to the call in your life. You are going to reach to the top. Yes, the very very top part of the best thing life has for you. You are going to claim it because it is yours and nobody else. It was determined for you and you alone. Nobody can claim it unless it is given to them by the owner, you! You are the one designated to overcome situational past, present and future. You are the model example for others to see. You are a trail blazer, friend until the end. This is your season to reap everything that you have sown. This is your **point of no return** to earn all that is due to you. Do not let your heart be discouraged or troubled when things do not seem right. Do not judge anything by the appearance of the elements in your life. They are designs to make you strong. Stay on course and pause for a minute when needed but never stop for too long. Remember that the race is not given to the fastest or the strongest but only the one that does not stop too long. Quickly regain self in the middle of strife and your struggles. Don't stay their long at all. If you do, you will begin to get so comfortable and lazy or dull of hearing. Believe me because I have been there and it does not take long to get comfortable and relax. You begin to dream and before you know it, time has passed. And you better believe the faithfulness of time. It does not wait even when we stop. I am not talking about the synthetic manmade materials on game day. Unfortunately, life is not a game friend as others seem to think. When we snooze, we lose and sometimes, it affects not only us but everyone else associated with us. Whether it is, not getting that well need education or job because I wasn't "proactive," it will crush and break many homes and lives as a whole. Whether it was because I did not "put first thing first" or just did not "begin with the end in mind," whatever excuse I may have had if I "let grass grow under my feet", it can be very detrimental to self and others. This is your **point of no return**. So you see, our lives are not just about self but we are the missing link to others. It is not just about me, me and me, alone. No, it is about your immediate family present or to be. It is about your neighbor and friends. It is about everyone you are going to meet. Do not under estimate your worth and potential in this world. Once again, let go of unnecessary weights that you have been carrying. Let them go for good. Let unresolved issues go and never received again. Kick doubts, out once and for all. Bitterness should be the reason for some of the stress in your life. Let them go so you can learn to flow and fly like the eagle you are. Anything in your life that cause you unwanted pressure, dismissed. You are greater than that. Relieve yourself of pain rendered by unwanted passengers. Received kindness and joy now in your life. Fear has not been fair to you now for a long time. It is the main reason you have not push and conquered that particular obstacle in your life. Break every chain and be loosed. For your time has come to unleashed the best in you. You are not the tail but you are the head of everything that is good and kind. You're exactly what you and others been waiting for, so believe it and live like it . You are the lender and not a borrower. Your life will never be the same anymore. You will not accept the curse or worst but you will step forward, now. It is your season; it is your time to shine. It's harvest time. The declaration of greatness has been spoken long time upon your life. It is your fate and destiny. The "son' will shine even though there are some stormy clouds ahead. "Lift your head towards the hills from whence your help cometh from." You have great people on your side.

You have great friends and family. Even if there are not many, whatever you have are there at your disposal. Use them wisely and you will succeed. This is your **point of no return.** Don't accept anything less but the best. Rise to the top and don't look back. Also watch how you treat others as you are going up, because you are going to have to face those same people on your way down. Treat your neighbors as you would want to be treated for truly this is a rule that's golden. Live by it and you will succeed even when they don't say please and thank you. What matters is that you kept your cool and you where not rude. Always be tender hearted for it's a friend that will stick closer than a brother. Be compassionate and life will be good to you. Excuse the unforgiveable and you will be forgiven. These are gold to the road of success and longevity. As much as possible, you must stay calm in your storms. Even when turbulence is at hand, remember you are the head and not the tail. As a matter of fact, be the peace others need in the midst of the storms. You are the types of materials pupils long to follow. This is your **point of no return** so don't look back. No matter what lies ahead, attack. Be strong for you are not alone. Be encouraged, for your victory is a head. This is your season for you have arrived at the **point of no return**!

This is your **Point of no return**. You're almost home; you are too far from Rome. It does not matter how things may appear, you hear! When all seems so insignificant and just not working right, remember the purpose you began first of all. Do not lose faith and hope in the purpose. If that your purpose was significant from the beginning, why should it change? Remember, that you have the merchandize to win again and again. Do not stop base on circumstances. Your fate is first not last; you will receive good and not evil because it is your expected end. Do not doubt your process through your test. Yes! Sometimes you will be tested and an unbearable ways, but who can go though better than you. Lift your eyes toward your hills from where your strengths come from. Do not forget that the Lord is on your side and you can do all things. No matter how strenuous it maybe, you are the head and not the tail. Take control of your situations by the horn and turn them around. Let not circumstances change your weather, never. The power to change and create your weather is yours. Most importantly, never under estimate the process of God to bring you over. I have never known God to start and don't come through. He specializes when it seems impossible. He is a mind regulator to those who pray every day. Remember this is the Point of no return. You are home bound and free to make it successfully. No matter how it seems and feels. Do not quit! Please do not throw in the towel, ever. You are one of a kind that was created in the image of greatness. You are imbedded with the spirit of limitless potentials and creativity. You are formed with light of understandable drive and destination, elevation point. You have fallen enough and have been too low but to go up now. You have paid your dues to disappointment, fully. Your account with sadness is a positive one. You have good credit with joy everlasting and happiness all the time. You are now free to be blessed and not stress. You are now free to enter glory land. You have arrived at a place of endless opportunities to choose from because you have worked hard and kept at it. Yes, you are at the point of no return. It is a place where light overwhelms dark thought of the mind. It is a place where a discouragement is dismissed for countless offense on lives of potential doctors and others. This is where the winds of negativity don't blow and pushes us against the odds. It is a place where the waves of humanity cannot toss us here and there, everywhere. It is your turn to create your own weather of deserving accomplishments. This is your season to harvest in all the joy for the relentless drive you have displayed time and time again. It is Celebration Avenue for you. It is your season to make it known that you are the head and not the tail. It is you time to lend and not borrow. Your storm is over now and you are seeing clearly now the rain is gone. Everything you went though was massive but worth it. It was worth the wait and hassle. All the pain was not easy but look at you now. Mr. and Mrs. Got it together now. Before you is an opened door! The universe is wide opened to conquer by you because greatness is inside you. You were born for to be royalty so won't be bound. Just do what you were meant to be. Just walk it and talk it. Only remember that because of the creator of heaven and earth, you are what you are. Never fail to acknowledge the God of heaven and earth and you'll be better than the best. Don't ever forget the river and stream of living water and your live will never run dried. This is your seasons of harvest and golden grain. You are made for this time and no one but you can stop you. Be bold and remember, nothing by any means can and will harm you as long as you stay in the hand of the man who can. No weapon designed can hurt you. But if by any chances, that situations may come your way, I want you to know that they are not given power at any given time to hurt you. Be it known to you that they are only designed to eliminate the obstacles in your life. Don't let any weight hold you down.

They are there to make sure that your every work is complete for you are not average. You are better than the best of them so realize the moment and just accomplish all that you were intended to be. You are, once again, the head and not the tail! You are a born leader. You are a trail blazer, friend. Make full proof of the merchandize within the content of your makeup. By no means should anything or anyone stand before you while the almighty is on your side because it is your season and **point of no return**. You are more than a conqueror through Christ who is with you. Do not let your members deceive you. Don't let them deny you of your opportunity of a life time. Be proactive and run this show, for sure. If you want this, just fix your eyes on the man who can. I wrote this sometime ago:

I know I can

Like a fan spinning

Again and again

It's real

No, I don't need a peal

To feel real

I don't need to make a deal

With the enemy of soul

It can grow pretty cold

And becomes old

so I prefer to stay with my God for he is good as gold!

That's right, with God we can't go wrong because it is the point of no return that you have yearn for. It is where everything flow and just glow. This is your season to reap what you have sawn. Hang on to the truths of your heart and don't ever part. No matter what may come your way, you will win. You are the next one in line. It is confirm and sealed. Lift your head up for the day of redemption is here. This is your **point of no return**.

Lightning Source UK Ltd.
Milton Keynes UK
UKHW020618050320
359822UK00011B/914

9 781977 221742

OZZY ANI

Joe Savage

The author of SEA TO BELIEVE

APS BOOKS
Yorkshire

APS Books,
The Stables Field Lane,
Aberford,
West Yorkshire,
LS25 3AE

APS Books is a subsidiary of the APS Publications imprint

www.andrewsparke.com

First published worldwide by APS Books in 2023

A catalogue record for this book is available from the British Library

OZZY AND SAMMY

I'm only doing this stupid thing because it was Miss Kaur who said that I should try it. It's kind of funny that my old Maths teacher said I should write a diary. She spoke to me today because she said the other teachers were worried about me. She said they noticed that I was quieter than usual, but aren't I always quiet? Anyway, she asked me if I was thinking about Lane Island again. I must've forgotten that she was there at the town hall when I did that speech. The truth is that I haven't thought about Lane Island in ages, even though I can't look out at the sea without seeing it. How long has it been since I went there? Two years? Man, where does the time go. A lot has happened since then. Mr Murphy restarted the scuba diving club not long after *the Unsinkable* was found and so I've managed to dive in the open sea a few more times since then. I don't see him that much anymore; I guess he's got a new group at the swimming pool and getting them ready to dive in the summer holiday. Mum is still working hard; she never really stops. Ben is good too. He stopped scuba diving because he's got a part-time job at the newsagents but we still meet up and walk along the cliffs after school when we have the time to. But Ozzy…forget it, this diary is stupid. I don't want to talk about what's happening to Ozzy.

Tuesday 7th February

I couldn't talk any more last night. I was already tired when I started talking because part of me didn't want to do it at all. I thought about deleting yesterday's entry but I went to sleep instead. I feel a little better this morning, but I'm annoyed I woke up early so I might as well carry on with this before school. Ozzy; well, something horrible happened to him last Saturday. He walked in from the garden and was about to go upstairs,

1

but he collapsed and started to breathe heavily. It only lasted about a minute, but I thought he was, I thought he was…

When it finished, he stood up and walked upstairs like nothing happened at all. I couldn't believe it. Mum phoned the vets and managed to get an emergency appointment that afternoon. The vet said Ozzy had a brain seizure and will need to take regular medication. I'm not sure what she gave him; I can't remember those long, scientific names for medicines. The vet also said that we should take Ozzy more often now to make sure he's okay. Ever since Saturday, every time I see Ozzy, I worry for him. I know he's getting old; I've known him almost all fifteen years of my life, but it doesn't make it easier knowing that he might not have much time left. I wish I could turn back time and relive everything again forever. I don't know life without him. I told all of this to Miss Kaur yesterday because I trust her, that's why she suggested to me to try writing this diary. I think she understands because she has a cat of her own. I want to talk to her again but I know she's busy with classes and stuff. Maybe I should try and talk to Ben about Ozzy today.

I've just come home from school. I managed to speak to Ben at lunchtime. He said he doesn't know what to say because he's never had a pet. At least he was honest with me. When I walked into my room, Ozzy was sleeping at the end of my bed. It reminded me of the morning after Mrs. Anderson cancelled my first scuba diving lesson in the sea: when I tried to walk downstairs but I ended up going back to bed. But then Ozzy walked into my room to sit with me for a while and it made me feel better. I wonder if he knew? I wish I could ask him. I'm looking at him right now, and I can't help but worry. Before Saturday, I would smile every time he snored, but now I'm afraid that he won't wake up again. Mum tried to put his medicine with his dinner, but he's somehow able to know exactly where the tablet is and only eats the food around it. So, I have to open his mouth as Mum gives him the tablet and rub his throat. It's not something I want to do, but I know it's to help Ozzy stay as healthy as he can right now. I think he understands though as he doesn't growl or bite us when we give him his medicine. He hasn't had another seizure since Saturday, and although I'm grateful for that, my brain keeps thinking about the next one. I hope it doesn't happen but I want to be able to help him if it does. I don't know what else to say right now. I'm not even sure if writing about it is helping me, to be honest. But I'll keep trying, I don't want to disappoint Ozzy by running away from this.

Wednesday 8th February

Ozzy was sick a few minutes ago, I think we gave him too many treats for taking his tablet. He didn't have a seizure though, so I'm grateful for that. It reminded me of the time he vomited on a book Mum was reading years ago. I think she was even close to finishing the book which made it even funnier! I swear I laughed for hours when I heard about what he did! When Mum told him off, I think he looked proud of what he achieved; he must not have liked that book at all! That's why I'm speaking about this straight away; I want to put it into words as it's fresh in my memory. Mum said he used to be sick in my room when I was really young. It must have been when he started to live with us because I don't remember it at all. That reminds me, I don't even know how old Ozzy is. I think I remember him when he was a kitten or a year old or something, but I don't know, to be honest. I wonder what he was like when he was very young. I wish I could remember so I could write more memories but I was barely even three when he first lived with us. Is that the time? I'm going to be late for school!

I'm saying this just before I go to bed because today was exhausting. I had to run to school because I was so focused on retelling the time Ozzy was sick in Mum's book. It was worth it though; it made school a bit more bearable. I was a little bit late but Mr Butler told me not to worry about it. I guess Miss Kaur told him about what's happening with Ozzy. I'm not

sure if I like people knowing what I'm going through or not, especially i
I'm not the one who's telling them. It makes me feel weak. Don't get m
wrong, I understand that Miss Kaur is trying to do what's best but, I don'
know. I just don't know. I think I need to talk to Mr Murphy again. I stil
haven't forgotten him telling me that he doesn't want me to be like him
Even though he wants me to be better than that, I don't know anyon
stronger than him. Well, maybe except Mum; I mean, he did teach her t
scuba dive when she was young. Maybe Mum learnt how to be stron
because of him. She doesn't seem phased by Ozzy's illness; she just give
him his tablet and then starts work. I wish I could do that; I wish I coul
just give him his medicine and go to school like nothing is happening
Maybe this diary is a weakness. Maybe telling Miss Kaur about Ozzy is ;
weakness. I think I need to sleep on it and see how I feel in the morning

Friday 10th February

Ben and I walked along the cliffs after school today. The weather was fine
I guess. He said that I was walking more quickly than usual. I said I wasn'
but, to tell the truth, I just wanted to go home to see if Ozzy was okay
He probably knows though; I did tell him about Ozzy's seizure after all
Besides, I don't want to worry him with troubles he can't help me with
that's not fair on him. Anyway, we bumped into Mr Murphy. I'm glac
Tipton-on-Sea is a small town. I think Mr Murphy could tell something
was wrong, so I explained what was going on with Ozzy. He reminde
me of the promise I kept to him about taking lots of photos with Ozzy.
did do that but I think I stopped after a while. I'm not even sure why
maybe I thought I had too many photos or something. I found the bo:
where I stored the photos Mum printed a couple of years ago. I'm lookin
at them right now in fact. There's one of me and Ozzy sitting at th
windowsill. I think I was waiting for Mr Murphy so we could go to th
library. Oh, this was a good one! It's Ozzy sitting on me when I fel

backwards through the front door! I was outside, leaning on the door as I looked out at the sea. Mum opened the door before I could stand up in time. I think Ozzy was more concerned about being comfortable than making sure I was okay! Still, it made for a good picture so I'm glad I got it. I don't know if I should take pictures of Ozzy right now. He looks more scruffy now than he does in the photos. I know he can't help it though. Nah, I let him sleep right now. Mum said he isn't going out into the garden much anymore. I'm hoping it's just because it's winter right now. I wish I could do something to save him; I hate feeling powerless. I think he has an appointment at the vet's next week. I'm going to go so I can be more useful. Yeah, I think that's the best thing I can do right now.

Saturday 11th February

Mr Murphy visited the house this morning. He said he had a little bit of time before starting one of his lessons at the swimming pool. Ozzy greeted him, he must've remembered him from a couple of years ago. Mr Murphy said I should help him with some of the lessons at the pool to help me take my mind off Ozzy. Mum said it was a good idea and asked for a copy of his timetable. I said I'd think about it but I already decided not to. I'd rather spend more time with Ozzy; if the worst was to happen and I wasn't around, I would never forgive myself. It's now been a week since his first seizure. I think he's his old self again but it's hard to tell anymore. The tablets seem to be working at least. I feel like I should be writing more in this diary, but I don't know what to say anymore. I think it's better to stop rambling and actually write when I have something to say.

Ozzy had another seizure. It happened not long after he had his lunch. I was sitting in the living room when he came through from the kitchen. Just like last time, he collapsed and started to breathe heavily. I sat with him through it all, but there was nothing I could do. After a couple of minutes, he got up and walked away. I didn't know what to say when it happened; I just sat on the carpet and watched him walk upstairs. I felt powerless again. I felt weak and to be honest, I still do. I can't talk to Mum about this. I don't know why. I mean, she saw Ozzy's seizure too. My only hope now is asking the vet what I can do to help Ozzy. His appointment is tomorrow afternoon, straight after school. I'm going to run home. I don't care how tired I am during the day. I need to run home. I should be playing a game right now, but I don't feel like it. Maybe I'll take a walk and look at the sea instead. I don't care that it's raining right now; I've walked through worse.

I've just got home. Ozzy greeted me at the door, I think he just woke up. I sat with him for a couple of minutes before I even took my coat off. I had a horrible thought as I was looking at the sea: what if the vet wants to put Ozzy to sleep? I couldn't move. I don't think I'm strong enough to face that possibility yet. I really hope it doesn't come to that.

Monday 13th February

Woke up early again. Even though I'm tired, I just couldn't get to sleep. So, I went downstairs to get his carrier ready before starting this entry. At least that way we won't have to rush before going to the vet's after school. Ozzy was sleeping when I walked downstairs. I saw him on the sofa as I was getting the carrier. Luckily, I was quiet enough not to wake him up; he's going to need all the rest he can get. I can't stop thinking about what might happen at the vet's, I have to try to prepare myself for the worst. I'm going to sit with him awhile before I have to go to school.

Just got home. I went in with Ozzy and Mum to see the vet. The vet said that Ozzy is doing okay despite his seizures. To say that I'm relieved is an overstatement…or is it understatement? I can never remember the difference. Anyway, I asked the vet how I can help Ozzy if he has another seizure. He said that I should try and make the room as quiet as possible by turning off the TV, computer and anything else I can control. I'm grateful that I now know how to help Ozzy, even if it only helps a little. I noticed that Ozzy was quiet when we put him in the carrier before going to the vet's. Even when we came home and opened his carrier, he just stayed in it for a few minutes before finally leaving. Either he's used to being in the carrier now or he just doesn't have the energy to fight back anymore. He used to meow all the time and try to claw his way out when he was younger. He actually used to be great at escaping when he was younger; I remember when he actually managed to claw the carrier door open when we first got it! I should've been annoyed, but I was actually impressed that he was able to do it. And then there was the time he managed to remove the cone from his head: he had to get a wound on his shoulder treated after fighting a stray cat in our garden years ago, and to stop him from licking the wound. I remember turning away for a few seconds and when I turned back to look at him, his cone was on the floor and he looked at me like he did nothing wrong! He's never tried to run away from home though, even when he managed to take his cone off when I wasn't looking. I guess that means he is happy living here. Maybe it's because we give him so many treats especially now. It's been a long day, I think I'll check on Ozzy before seeing if I have any homework to do for tomorrow, even though I don't see the point of having to do it.

I had a good sleep last night; it must have been because of the long day yesterday. I gave Ozzy his breakfast but he refused to eat it. I was worried until I realised that he knew it wasn't the expensive food! He certainly is picky now! So, I gave him the top-quality brand and he quickly ate it. Usually, I'd be annoyed that he wasted food, but I can't be mad at him, not anymore. Besides, I guess it's my fault that I got him that free sample from the supermarket a few months ago; he rarely ate anything else since. Still, he deserves it for helping me feel better when I was feeling ill or just not feeling good at all. He would always stay by my side if I was in bed with a massive headache or cold or something. I guess that's why I want to return the favour by staying with him through this. If it was up to me, I would skip school entirely so I could keep an eye on him all day, but all I can do is rush home after school as quickly as I can.

It's 9 PM right now. I've just spent the last hour or so searching for Ozzy. Even Mum was worried, I searched the house, the garden, even the street at the front of the house. I found him hiding under the sink, somewhere he never used as a hiding place before. I remember reading that cats hide away when they are seriously ill to protect themselves from predators. If so, it makes sense that Ozzy didn't look happy to see me, I can't explain why I think that it's just a - what's the word? - instinct, I guess.

Wednesday 15th February

I decided to leave Ozzy where he was. I didn't want to cause him more stress. I tried to tempt him out with his favourite food, but he wouldn't budge. I ended up taking his food to him. I know he likes to be treated from time to time, but that was taking the mick! I'm glad he ate it though. I guess that's a sign that he's getting better. I bumped into Miss Kaur at lunch time; she asked how Ozzy was doing but I couldn't tell her the truth. It hurts too much. So, I told her that he's doing okay. That's it. I don't think she believed me, but to be honest, it doesn't matter. If I have to go to school, I don't want to be reminded about Ozzy from others. I just want to go in, do what I have to do and then come home. When I did get home, he was still under the sink. Mum was working from home again; she said Ozzy didn't move when she went downstairs to check. It isn't what I wanted to hear at all. He was sleeping, I know he was because I checked his breathing when I gave him his dinner, so I just left it beside him. I'll check if he's eaten it before I go to bed. I just hope he wakes up.

Thursday 16th February

I woke up to find Ozzy sitting on the end of my bed. Either he sneaked in or I was in a deep sleep because I certainly didn't hear him jump on my bed. Who knows how long he stayed there? Anyway, I'm just happy he's moved out of the cupboard under the sink. That means he's getting better, right? So, I went downstairs to give him his breakfast and he followed closely behind me. Then…the nastiest smell hit my nose! I squeezed my nose as hard as I could and ran to his litter tray in the hallway, it was the biggest…poo I had ever seen! It looked like a yule log! And guess who had to clean it up? It's not exactly how I imagined starting the day, especially with Ozzy staring at me as I put fresh litter in his box. I swear he was laughing as I carried the bag to the bin in the garden. When I came back in, I sprayed as much deodorant as possible in the hallway. Ozzy…of course…stood by his bowl and acted like he didn't just lay the world's biggest turd! But the important thing is that he is moving and eating again, so at least I can go to school without worrying as much. Ozzy's next appointment will be coming up soon, I wonder if it's worth telling the vet that Ozzy hid a couple of days ago. I'll think about it as I'm walking to school.

Saturday 18th February

Ozzy had another seizure this morning. I think they are happening more often now. I turned the TV off and stayed as quiet as possible, just like the vet told me to. This time was different though; as he lay on the floor still panting, he did another massive poo. I wonder if the same one he did a couple of days ago was because of a seizure. Part of me thinks so, but the other part hopes it wasn't because he did it in his litter tray. I don' know what to do. Staying by his side doesn't feel like I'm doing enough I can't help but wonder how much he's suffering. I wish I knew for sure because I don't want him in pain. It's all so confusing. Ben and I were going to walk on the cliffs today but…I don't want to do it anymore. I've got to stay with Ozzy in case he has another seizure. Mum told me to go with Ben because she will stay at home, but I know she's busy. She's always busy. Anyway, I'm going to keep an eye on Ozzy now. I'm not sure when I'll write next.

Wednesday 22nd February

It isn't fair. I forgot to do my homework for Geography on Monday, the only time I ever have, and I was forced to stay after school today for punishment. I had to sit in silence until I did my homework. What is the point? I've got far more important problems to deal with, but instead I had to sit and write something that won't even matter when I leave school for good. I hate this place. I hate being forced to go when Ozzy is getting worse. Ben met me outside the gate when I was finally free. He wanted to know if I was okay. I told him the exact same thing I wrote here. He didn't respond, he didn't even try to crack one of the terrible jokes he learnt from his dad. I don't know why he bothered waiting if he had nothing to say to me. I ended up just walking off; I just wanted to get home. When I did get home, Ozzy was sleeping on the floor in the living room. I wanted to sit with him for a while but I didn't want to wake him up. So, I just opened the back door and sat on the step for a while. I didn't see the stray cat until he walked up to me. He's a beautiful tabby and white that started showing up not long after we found *the Unsinkable*. I really should've given him a name by now. Anyway, I think he was waiting for Ozzy to come out because they always hang out in the garden…well…they used to anyway. I gave him some of Ozzy's treats, just like I always do, but he still waited for Ozzy to come out. I had to close the door when he tried to come into the house, I really didn't want to but I couldn't risk him disturbing Ozzy. He kept meowing at the door, but what else could I do? Ozzy has another appointment on Saturday. I need to ask the vet if there is anything else I can do to help Ozzy get better.

Sunday 26th February

I overslept yesterday, so Mum took Ozzy to the vets by herself. I was angry when I woke up to a text from her saying they were there. She phoned not long after saying his appointment went well and she was waiting for a taxi to take them home. All I could do was sit and wait. After about half an hour, there was a massive knock on the door. I ran as quickly as I could to open it. Mum barged past me and put the carrier on the floor. Ozzy…Ozzy was screaming in pain. I raced to open the carrier and help him get out. He took a few steps before collapsing and panting with his head on the floor. I tried to stay with him but I couldn't bear seeing him in pain. So…I ran upstairs like a coward. I curled up on my bed and covered my ears, but I could still hear him screaming. I should've stayed with him, but all I did is shout in my head like a coward. When he started to have seizures, I kept pleading for him to get better. But when I heard his screams, I pleaded to something, anything, I pleaded: 'please end his suffering', and with that, the screaming stopped. I could hear Mum walking up the stairs, so I walked down the hallway to meet her. Her eyes were red and she told me:

"I'm sorry…Ozzy's gone."

I tried so hard to stay strong, but I cried. I cried so much. There are still tear stains on the carpet now. Somehow, I made it downstairs and I saw him lying on the floor. I kneeled beside him and stroked his head, hoping that he would wake up and purr…but he didn't. Mum wiped her tears and told me that she's going to phone the vet. I couldn't say anything, even if I wanted to. I just stayed with Ozzy while I could. Mum went into the living room and closed the door, I'm grateful she gave me a chance to say my last goodbyes to Ozzy. I told him that I love him and I'm sorry I wasn't there for him. Ozzy helped me so many times through all my life that I hate myself for not returning the favour when he needed it the most. I conquered my fears at Lane Island and the town hall so why couldn't I do it here? Ozzy deserved so much better than me. Mum opened the living room door and told me the taxi was on the way. I kissed Ozzy's head and gently wrapped him in the blanket from his carrier. Mum took off the lid of the carrier so I could place Ozzy in gently. Mum and I sat in silence either side of Ozzy. It felt like forever before the taxi arrived but a part of me was grateful because it didn't want to let Ozzy go. We heard a car driving up the road and so Mum opened the front door to check. It was the taxi. Mum asked me if I was coming but I told her I can't. I can cry at home but I can't in public. I think Mum understood. I slowly picked up the carrier and passed it to her; I didn't want to believe that I would never see Ozzy again, I still don't. I walked with Mum to the taxi, trying to stop myself from shaking as I opened the car door. I said goodbye to Mum and Ozzy and watched the taxi drive off. And that was it. I walked back into my house and closed the front door. I'll never forget how quiet it was. It was completely silent. I've never heard it so quiet before, not even when Mum used to take Ozzy for his appointments. I felt…lost. That's when I remembered the time Ozzy disappeared years ago. Mum and I went on holiday to Wales for a week and stayed with an old friend of hers. Mrs Corbett from next door came round a few times a day to check on Ozzy and give him his food and water. When we got home, we let Ozzy go out. After a few hours, I checked to see if he was in the garden. I couldn't see him anywhere. I looked over the fences into next-door's garden and he wasn't there either. To be fair, it wasn't unusual if he stayed out a little longer than normal; he would sometimes roam the street on warm nights. But in the morning, he still wasn't home. I checked the garden again, I checked round the front, I even walked up and down the street to try and find him. Mrs. Corbett said she hadn't seen Ozzy either. That was the first time I noticed how quiet the house could be and I didn't like it. The day he was missing felt like a lifetime; at least it did back then. I don't know how many times I ran up to my bedroom window to see if he came back. On the second day, I ran to the window as soon as I woke up to see if he was outside. But he wasn't. I checked around the front again, walked up and down the street. Nothing. No sign of him. The second day he was missing dragged on too. In the evening, maybe about 5 or 6, I went out in the garden and shouted for Ozzy one more time. I heard something jump up the fence right at the bottom of the garden. Ozzy slowly strolled up the fence looking smug like he was pretending he hadn't been home for two days. He jumped onto the path and walked right past me as I stared at him. Crazy. The difference between back then and now is that back then I always had hope that he would come home. In a way, I wanted to go into the garden once I got home today and shout for Ozzy again. But there's no point. He won't be coming home any more. So, I ran upstairs to my room and slammed the door shut. I sat on my bed and stared at the computer, part of me wanted to write this all down, but I think it would've been a big mess. I'm still finding it hard to get past this, and the worst part is I've got to go to school tomorrow and pretend everything is fine, I don't want to think about this anymore. I wish this was just a bad dream that I will wake up from. I want to see Ozzy happy and healthy. Is that too much to ask for?

Today was horrible. I left the house and people greeted me as I walked to school. I had to fight to smile back and say hello back. I don't know if they noticed, I walked too quickly to check. When I got to school, I saw everyone playing football, laughing or doing last-minute homework. I never thought it would be strange seeing everyone being normal. That's when I realised that the world is moving on without me. I didn't feel like talking to anyone, so I hid in an empty corner of the playground until the bell rang. Morning classes were weird; I don't remember much about the lessons themselves but none of the teachers asked me questions and they didn't ask for my homework. I can't deny I was happy that they left me alone though; I needed that today. Miss Kaur came to find me at break time. She said, "I'm truly sorry, Sammy. If you ever need to talk, I'll be in the staff room after school." All I could do was look down and nod. When I looked up again, Ben was standing in front of me, and the memories of Lane Island came flooding back. I began to breathe heavily, just like I did in my scuba mask. Ben looked like he was struggling too, just like I did when I stood between him and the pit, and then he said, "Sammy, I, er, so, when are you going to get a new cat?" I clenched my fist and punched him in his face. He fell to the floor as blood from his nose sprayed my face and shirt. I had never punched anyone before in my whole life, and the last person I ever wanted to was Ben, but I couldn't believe my best friend would disrespect me and Ozzy like that. Before I knew it, everyone gathered round and chanted, "Fight! Fight! Fight!" I couldn't move; I was still trying to understand what I done. Miss Kaur broke through the crowd and stood between me and Ben. I'll never forget the look of disappointment on her face. Ben slowly stood up and stared at me, I couldn't tell if he was angry or shocked because he had his hand covering his left eye, nose and mouth. If he was going to punch me back, I would've accepted it. But he didn't try to punch me; he just shook his head and walked away. Everyone else walked away soon after, everyone apart from me and Miss Kaur. She quietly told me, "We need to see Mr Wyatt." I just nodded and slowly walked beside her. Miss Kaur knocked on the door of the Headteacher's office and Mr Wyatt told us to walk in. All I could do was look at the floor as Miss Kaur explained what she saw. She also said that my Mum phoned the school to say that Ozzy passed away yesterday. I clenched my fists again without even thinking about it. Mr Wyatt asked Miss Kaur to bring Ben in to explain what happened. In all the time Miss Kaur was away, I never once looked up and Mr Wyatt never said a word to me. When Ben came in, he sat as far away from me as possible. I don't blame him. He told Mr Wyatt everything that happened and explained that he didn't know what to say when he overheard Miss Kaur talking to me about Ozzy. My heart sank. Ben never had any pets and he was just trying to help me. His dad was right, Ben and I were like brothers...but I've lost that now, and it's all my fault. Mr Wyatt asked me if I had anything to say, but I was still frozen in place. He told me that I was being sent home for the rest of the day. I didn't complain, I just wish he did that before Ozzy died. Mr Wyatt phoned Mum at work and told her what happened. He then told me to gather my things and go home. Miss Kaur escorted me to the front gates and asked me if I had been keeping a diary. I just nodded. She asked me if she could read it when it's done. I'm not sure I want to share it with anyone. I don't want anyone to treat me differently because of this diary. But if it wasn't for Miss Kaur, I wouldn't have kept this diary in the first place. I walked up to the cliffs on the way home and sat down to watch the sea. It felt like Lane Island was watching me. I felt cold, even colder than this winter. I looked to my left and saw a bag of sweets, and next to it was Ben, but he was younger. The last thing I need is my mind reminding me of what I've lost. I ran away, wanting to get home as quickly as possible. As soon as I opened the door, everything was silent. It started to dawn on me that I would have to get used to this. Ozzy won't be home to greet me anymore. He won't be here when I wake up anymore. He won't be scratching my door when I'm upset or ill anymore. The only things that show he lived here are his food and bowls. I'm not ready to live like that. I needed more time. It isn't fair. All I could do is sit on the back step and look out at the garden as I try to gather my thoughts. Then, I saw the stray running down the path and calling for Ozzy. I started to stroke him to calm him down but I had to stop because it felt...I don't know, it just didn't seem right after what happened with

Ozzy. The stray just sat in front of me and stared, I think he was still waiting for Ozzy. I wish I could get him to understand, but then again maybe it's for the best that he doesn't know. I ended up just giving him treats and closed the back door. I messaged Mum to say I got home before sitting down in the living room to watch the TV. I kept expecting to hear Ozzy walk down the stairs to sit and watch with me, or just scratch the settee if he woke up in a bad mood. At least he left us something to remember him by. Every time I heard a creak upstairs, I'd turn to look and think he's coming down. The hours dragged on until Mum got home. I braced myself for the worst, thinking she would shout and scream because I was sent home…but she did what she always does: shut down and not talk to me at all. She took the remote, sat down on the settee and put on a song. It was 'Who Knew' by *P!nk*. She didn't say a word as it played; she just stroked the arm rest where Ozzy left some scratch marks. I tried to fight it, but I couldn't help but cry with her, the song perfectly told me what I was feeling. When it finished, Mum told me that she played it at work today when she couldn't stop thinking about Ozzy on her break. All I could do was sit in silence and listen to her. She told me that listening to music like this is how she mourns and she thinks it will help me too. It's honestly a relief to know that I'm not suffering alone, and now I understand why I can't move on yet: it's not because Ozzy was gone, it's because I don't want to forget him. I told Mum that I understand…but that's when she asked me about Ben.

She wanted to know why I punched him. All I could say was the truth: I thought he was disrespecting Ozzy and I was stupid for thinking so, but it's too late now. She told me not to think like that just yet and I should actually try to talk to him. But I don't think he'll talk to me…I wouldn't talk to me. I didn't want to talk about it anymore, so I went to my room to write about today. I wish it wasn't so long, but something is telling me that I need to write this so I don't forget.

I messaged Ben last night telling him I was sorry for punching him and that I know he was only trying to make me feel better, even though he doesn't know what I'm going through. And…I said that if he never wants to talk to me again, I understand. He didn't respond. I don't even think he's seen the message. Either way, I'll stay away from him today. I went downstairs as soon as I woke up to give Ozzy his breakfast. It was only when I grabbed his bowl when I realised that I couldn't feed him anymore. I froze in place until Mum saw me. She told me it's time to put his things away. As much as it hurt seeing his bowl empty, I think it will hurt more putting it somewhere I'll forget. I desperately tried to think of an excuse to keep his things. 'What about letting the stray use it?' I thought, and then I told Mum. To my surprise, she agreed with me. So, Ozzy's food and dish will be used for the stray now. At least there's that. Speaking of the stray, he was out this morning so I gave him the last of the treats before getting ready to go to school. I'm not sure how long I'm staying; I've got a meeting with Mr Wyatt to see if I'm allowed back to school. Mum has the morning off work for this. Hopefully, it won't take too long.

Just got home from school. I didn't see Ben. A part of me was happy, but the other wanted to try to apologise to him and make things right. Mum told Mr Wyatt what we talked about last night, I just stared at the floor the whole time. Mr Wyatt asked me what I wanted to do: whether I wanted to come back or not. Before I could answer, Mum told Mr Wyatt that she wanted me back in school tomorrow. I couldn't believe it. School wasn't a priority now I lost Ozzy and my best friend. Before I could say anything, Mr Wyatt agreed and the meeting ended. I glared at Mum just like I did to Mr Murphy before my second dive. I'm getting really tired of decisions about me where I don't have a say. I didn't speak to Mum on the way home. I still haven't to be honest. I just ran upstairs to my room and decided to write this. It feels weird to say this, but I think keeping this diary is finally helping me. I don't know why, but I'm feeling calmer as I write this. I guess Miss Kaur was right.

Wednesday 1st March

Just woke up, went downstairs and picked up Ozzy's bowl again. I'm glad the stray came round early today so I could use the bowl. He still tries to come in the house. I still feel bad about having to keep him out, but there's no way I'm going to have another cat again. It hurts too much. Anyway, I better get ready for school. It's not like I have a choice anymore.

Just got home. The teachers quietly asked me if I did my homework, I just shook my head and they left me alone. I'm not sure how much longer that's going to last, so I can't push my luck. Ben and I sat on opposite sides of the classroom. I still don't know if he's read my message or not, but there's nothing more I can do. So, I just did what I could do in the lesson and went out to break. I sat on my own in the corner thinking of a song I can dedicate to Ozzy. Then Rose, one of my classmates, came up to me and said that she heard about Ozzy. I asked her how she knew, and she said Ben told her. I felt numb. Rose then told me that her dog, Rover, passed away a few months ago, and she was still mourning him. I looked up to her and said "I'm sorry to hear that." She just nodded and stood still. I think if I found out at any other time, I would've sat with her for a while and ask if she wanted to talk about Rover. But in that moment, the last thing I wanted to talk about were pets. I think Rose took the hint that I wasn't ready to talk, as she left after a few seconds. I stayed in the corner until the end of break. The rest of the lessons went pretty much the same. I don't know what else to say.

I didn't think I'd write anymore tonight, but the stray had other ideas. He was meowing constantly in the garden about an hour ago and I feared the worst. As soon as I opened the backdoor, he rolled around on the path and tried to look as cute as possible. He was just hungry. I closed the door and got Ozzy's bowl and put some treats in. I opened the door again and as soon as put the bowl down, the stray bolted into the house from my left! He ran straight into the kitchen and I followed him as quickly as I could, accidentally kicking the bowl as I turned around. I knew it was going to be a long night. The stray hid under the table and hissed at me before running into the living room. He ran around in circles and jumped up on the chairs and settee, he knocked down ornaments and teacups when he ran into the tables before finally hiding behind the TV. Luckily, the living room door was closed so he couldn't have access to the rest of the house...until Mum came downstairs and opened the door. The stray ran straight passed her and went upstairs. I told Mum what was happening and we went up to try and get the stray out of the house. I couldn't help but think of a few weeks ago when Ozzy hid away from us, so Mum and I checked the same places as we did with Ozzy. We ended up finding the stray in my room, hiding under my computer table. I tried to pick him up but he hissed at me again, so Mum went downstairs to grab the bowl from the garden and call him down. Surprisingly, it didn't work. What I ended up doing was shaking the table to scare him out and Mum guided him out of the house and back into the garden. I wonder what Ozzy would've made of it; I think he would've helped the stray cause as much mayhem in the house as possible. To be honest, I think I would've loved every second of it. But right now, I don't feel like laughing.

Thursday 2nd March

The stray was out early again. He kept meowing in the garden and I could hear him from my bedroom window. I guess he's my new alarm clock now. Luckily, we still had some of Ozzy's food left. I can't even begin to think what the stray would've done if we didn't. He tried to charge in as soon as I opened the backdoor; he would've worn his food if I lost my balance! But it was especially cold this morning, so I don't blame him for wanting to be inside, even after the carnage he caused last night. I made use of the time to catch up on any homework I missed. I can't push my luck, especially with the geography homework. Speaking of which, the homework is about Lane Island; can you believe it? If I don't get top marks on it, I'll call Mr Murphy and ask him to complain! That reminds me, I should go to the pool and help him with the scuba diving lessons; I can't keep staying home in complete silence. I guess I should speak to Rose too. As for Ben, he still hasn't messaged me. I guess that means he's made his mind up.

Just got home, I don't have long as I think the lesson at the pool starts at 6pm...at least it did when I took them years ago. I spoke to Rose at lunchtime today. She was in the corner first. I don't know whether she was waiting for me, but we talked about Ozzy and Rover straight away. She told me how Rover would always tear up her homework as a puppy and I told her about Ozzy always being sick on mine. It felt good knowing our pets hated homework as much as we did! I think it's the first time I've laughed all week. We shared a few more memories before the bell rang. I handed in my geography homework, just got to wait on the result. That's all I can write for now.

Just got back from the lesson at the pool. Mr Murphy didn't know I was coming so all I could do was sit and watch the lesson. It was strange being back at the pool; it looked so much bigger when I had lessons here. One of the kids struggled to put his mask on, so my instinct told me to go over and help him. He looked nervous as I approached and kneeled by him and it didn't even occur to me that I didn't ask Mr Murphy if I could help. When I looked at him, he just stared blankly at me and then nodded before passing me a spare mask. I slowly put it on to show how to do it for the kid and then got him to copy me. Luckily, it worked, and he was in the pool in no time. I spent the remaining time watching Mr Murphy teach. All the memories of my training came flooding back to me: the first time I tried to put on the diving suit, the first time Ben joined after I convinced him and the excitement I felt when Mr Murphy told us we were finally ready to dive at sea. I was so focused on the memories, that Mr Murphy had to snap me back to reality and see if I was okay! He asked if I had time to talk about Ozzy, and that's when I realised that I hadn't thought about Ozzy whilst I was watching the scuba diving lesson. I'm not sure whether that's a good or bad thing. I nodded, though part of me didn't want to talk about Ozzy. Mr Murphy asked me to carry some of the equipment back to his car before we sat down in the staff room of the swimming pool. He made me a cup of tea, just like he did after my first dive at sea, and asked me how I was feeling about Ozzy. I didn't even know where to begin; so much has happened to me since Sunday. I spent ages trying to find the right words, so Mr Murphy asked me if I remembered to take as many pictures and videos of Ozzy as I could. I told him that I obviously remember. He then asked me if I did. I didn't know how to answer, the best I could come up with was: as many as I could. He just responded "Good." I then remembered him telling me about his cat a couple of years ago, so I asked him about her. He said that her name was Mrs Happy and she lived to an old age like Ozzy. He told me she was a stray that would hang around the Lifeguard Headquarters and he would feed her every time he was down there and she would always try to follow him home. One day, he couldn't say no to her big green eyes and so he took Mrs Happy to his home. He said that she would eat her food as quickly as possible which probably meant that she was a stray all her life. Mr Murphy then went really quiet, even more quiet than normal. He told me that Mrs Happy passed away suddenly a year later. She had a tumour that grew overnight and there was nothing that the emergency vet could do to save her. I was in complete shock; I couldn't even imagine someone being fine one day and gone the next. In a weird way, I'm grateful now that I knew Ozzy was poorly. It feels so strange writing that. All I could say to Mr Murphy was that I'm sorry. I think he appreciated that because he smiled and said he was happy he gave Mrs Happy a warm home at the end of her life and he has many photos of her to look back at and smile. He then said that even though he only saw Ozzy a couple o times, he could see that Ozzy lived a good life. He then asked me if would change anything. I had so many thoughts that it felt like I woulc give the wrong answer no matter what I said. So, I gave the answer thought was the most right: "No, I wouldn't change anything." But know for sure that I can't do it again; I can't get another cat. It would hur too much knowing how it could end. Mr Murphy said he understood; he has taken in stray cats most of his life and knows the pain all too well. thought he would tell me that: 'time heals all wounds' or some othe rubbish and I'd eventually get another cat. But instead, he told me that he respects my decision to never get another cat again. I asked him why he takes in cats after his last ones had passed away. He clarified that he didn' get a new cat straight away; he sometimes waited a few months or even a few years; it all depended on how he was feeling. He then told me tha giving a home to older cats, who might not have long left, makes him happy. I was surprised he gave such a simple answer. Usually Mr Murphy goes into detail when talking about what he does and why. He then askec me how Ben was, as he hadn't seen Ben for a while. I really didn't wan to say what happened but I know Mr Murphy would instantly know if wasn't being honest. As I explained what happened on Monday, M Murphy stayed silent all the way through. He told me that I reminded him of the time he and Mr Green had a fight during a party at Old Merchant He didn't say much about it because he said it was decades ago and so he doesn't remember the details. Although, something tells me he does remember but he doesn't want to talk about it. Anyway, he said they didn' speak for years after the fight but eventually he felt like he had to get back in touch with Mr Green and make amends. I think he was trying to tell me that it will take years for Ben and me to be friends again. It certainly wasn't what I wanted to hear. But if that's what it takes, I can wait. It wa: starting to get late, so I said goodbye to Mr Murphy and made my way home to write all of this down straight away. Just before I walked out, he asked me if I was going to help with the lesson next week. I said yes. It' been a long day, but I'm glad I did what I did. I still have a long way to go, but I hope I'm making progress.

I feel so much better this morning. I think that I'll help the scuba diving club as much as possible. It gives me a purpose and ensures that I don't have to stay in a silent house when Mum is at work. This might be my last diary entry; I don't think I need this anymore. The stray was meowing before my alarm again. I'm not sure whether to thank him or start wearing ear plugs when I go to sleep. After I gave him his breakfast, I started listening to songs for Ozzy. Top 10, new artists; every playlist I listened to didn't have anything I thought was right; I don't think anything could top *P!nk's* 'Who Knew'. I guess it doesn't help that I never really paid attention to music growing up. It was always there in films and things but I was never interested in it. Anyway, I better get off to school.

Well, today was interesting. Rose told me a funny story of Rover stealing someone's dinner during a walk. Basically, Rose was walking Rover through the park and when they got to the top of the hill, Rover bolted over the top and Rose had to chase him. Rover returned with a sausage roll in his mouth! Turns out Rover stole it from a family having a picnic! Rose laughed as she told the story but she said that she was extremely embarrassed at the time. The story reminded me of all the times Ozzy stole chicken off my plate for Sunday dinner. I told Rose about the time Ozzy outsmarted me as I tried to hide my plate from him: sometimes, I would eat dinner in the living room and Ozzy would crouch and stalk my food like a lion. When we were younger, he was always faster than me and could always steal a piece of my chicken and escape before I could do anything! But as we got older, I got smarter…at least I thought I did. I would turn the plate so the chicken was closest to me and then I would hover my hands over so Ozzy didn't have an opening. After a while, Ozzy would give up and leave, and then I could eat in peace. Just as I was about to put my fork in the chicken, Ozzy swooped in from the left and grabbed the biggest piece of chicken from my plate! Thinking about it now, I wonder if Ozzy taught the stray how to be sneaky. Anyway, Rose and I had a good laugh; I never thought I'd look back and smile about my food being stolen, but I guess that's the best way I can describe my time with Ozzy. Rose and I were so deep in memory lane that we didn't notice Miss Kaur standing and watching us talk. She said she wanted to join in on the conversation but didn't want to disturb the funny stories we were telling. For some reason, I told Miss Kaur that I had finished the diary. Clearly, I hadn't as I'm writing this now! I guess it's because I plan to go and help out the scuba diving classes every Thursday. Anyway, Miss Kaur looked surprised and asked when she could read it. Before I could answer, Rose said, "You did a diary too?" Turns out, Rose spoke to Miss Kaur when Rover passed away. Rose then asked if she could read my diary too and she would let me read hers. I froze. Although I enjoyed my talks with Rose, I don't really know her. With our talks, I have control over what I want to say. I tried to think of the right way to say 'no thanks', but I just couldn't find it. Miss Kaur must've seen that I didn't want to swap diaries, as she stepped in and said that perhaps sharing happy stories is the better choice. I was obviously relieved, but Rose gave a smile and nodded. I could sense that she wasn't happy though. Luckily the bell rang. But as Rose began to walk away, I felt like I had to make sure we could still have these talks about Ozzy and Rover. I asked her if we can share more stories on Monday, she sighed and said, "Sure," before walking inside. Just as I was about to walk back into school, Miss Kaur asked me to wait a minute. She said that, although she still wants to read my diary, she will respect my decision to keep it private. All I could say was, "Thank you." I guess, now I'm writing this all down, I realise that mourning has no finish line. Maybe one day I will share this diary with Miss Kaur, Rose and even Ben. But for now, I feel like I'm ready to finish this diary. I'm already looking forward to helping the scuba diving club next week and sharing more stories with Rose. I'm even looking forward to waking up and giving the stray his breakfast, even if he keeps trying to get into the house. On Sunday, I'll eat my dinner in the living room as I listen to 'Who Knew' by P!nk, maybe I'll even leave a bit of chicken on the side of my plate.

Goodbye, Ozzy. I'll never forget you.

Printed in Great Britain
by Amazon

36652555R00020